The Easter Experience

For all the children at St Peter's 10:45 Express
You teach me so much!

Published by
The Bible Reading Fellowship
First Floor, Elsfield Hall
15–17 Elsfield Way, Oxford OX2 8FG
ISBN 1 84101 219 X

First published 2002
10 9 8 7 6 5 4 3 2 1 0

Acknowledgments
Unless otherwise stated, scripture quotations are taken from the Good News Bible published by The Bible Societies/HarperCollins*Publishers* Ltd, UK © American Bible Society 1966, 1971, 1976, 1992, used with permission.

A catalogue record for this book is available from the British Library.

Printed and bound in Great Britain by Omnia Books Ltd, Glasgow.

Beginning with God

The Easter Experience

Exploring the Bible with 5–7s

Rachel Heathfield

Contents

Week Four

Week Five

Welcome to The Easter Experience!

The death and resurrection of Jesus are central to the Christian faith and children need to understand them as much as adults. Wouldn't it be nice if we could read one section of the Bible and fully comprehend what it was all about? But we know this isn't the case.

Growing in faith and understanding of God is a bit like completing a jigsaw puzzle. Many different pieces are required to complete the picture; for most people those pieces are collected at different times and different places and are fitted together at yet another time.

As you and your child work through this book together, you will gather pieces for the jigsaw that shows us God's love for his people. We will look at what God plans and wants for his people, and we will look at forgiveness and new life and the events leading up to the first Easter.

Our hope is that this material will not simply be information gathering or totally knowledge-based. Our prayer is that as knowledge and understanding are gained, so personal faith in the Lord will grow. Collecting the jigsaw pieces is the first part of the process; completing the puzzle and believing what you see is just as important.

The material is divided into five weekly parts, with each part having up to six sessions. You could use the material on a daily basis (with one day a week 'spare') or work through the material at your own pace. You might find Week 3 and 4 particularly helpful in the fortnight leading up to Easter and Week 5 for the week after the Easter weekend. You choose!

Within each session there are five elements:

Looking back: helps you to reflect together about the day just gone and to give you something or someone to pray for.

To talk about: gives some open questions designed to get you thinking about the subject area for the session. There are no right or wrong answers here; sometimes you might have flowing conversation, at other times it might be shorter.

To do: gives something to do, either now or at a later stage; again this will contribute to your understanding of the Bible passage.

Explore the Bible: the verse is given in full for you to read together, with a short explanation after it. At this point you might like to make links with the earlier parts of the session.

Prayer jotter: the final part is for your child to reflect and pray on their own; the prayer journal encourages them to think about what you have just looked at together and to draw or write about it.

Spending time with your child like this is a privilege; may God bless you in it and bring you both pleasure and joy.

Rachel Heathfield

Holy God

Looking back

What do you enjoy doing in the time you're not at school? Playing with friends? Making things? Reading? Watching TV?

Thank God for those things.

To talk about

I wonder if you have ever been annoyed by something clean or new being spoilt by something dirty or old. Perhaps new, fresh paint spoilt by a dirty brush. Perhaps a clean T-shirt gets some food down it. Can you think of other examples of things being spoilt?

Explore the Bible

> **Everything you do, O God, is holy.**
>
> *Psalm 77:13*

God is holy. This is a word that means he is pure and unspoilt. He is a bit like fresh paint or a clean T-shirt: nothing dirty has ever spoilt him. Everything he does is good and fresh and new.

But people do wrong things every day. Wrong things are like a dirtiness that spoils us. It is impossible for us to be unspoilt all by ourselves.

To do

Here are some things that have been spoilt. Can you work out how they were spoilt?

Prayer jotter

Here are some things that are unspoilt. Think about the ways in which they might be spoilt and talk to God about it. Perhaps you could draw some more.

Dirty clothes

Looking back

What is the best thing you've worn over the last few days? Why do you like it?

Thank God that you have clothes to wear.

To do

Here are some pairs of things that are nearly the same. Draw lines between the pairs to link them up.

To talk about

What makes you and your class different from other classes at school? What separates you?

What separates you and your friends when you go home? What makes you different?

What marks out different gardens and houses? What keeps them separate?

Explore the Bible

> **Be merciful to me, O God, because of your constant love.**
>
> *Psalm 51:1*

The things we do wrong are like a hedge or a wall or a road that keeps us separate from God. Perhaps you can imagine the wrong things that we do being a bit like wearing dirty clothes—we are spoilt all over. You wouldn't wear dirty clothes if you were going to see someone really important, would you?

It is the wrong things that we do (like dirty clothes) that keep us separate from God.

Prayer jotter

Draw a face showing how you feel about God. Draw another face showing how God feels about you.

Kept apart

Looking back

Who are your friends? Name them to God now, asking him to look after them.

Are there things that are worrying your friends? Tell God about those things on their behalf. Ask him to help your friends.

To talk about

What upsets you? What do other people do that upsets you?

What makes you cross and angry? Think of times you have been cross.

What makes your parents or friends cross or upset?

Explore the Bible

I recognize my faults; I am always conscious of my sins. I have sinned against you—only against you—and done what you consider evil.

Psalm 51:3 and 4

The wrong things we do are called sins. Wrong things make God feel really upset. This is mostly because they keep us and God apart.

The person who wrote these verses was a king called David. We read about him in the Old Testament. Mostly he was a really good king. But he knew he had upset God by doing something wrong. He was sad that his sin had upset other people, but most of all he was sad that he had upset God.

To do

Match the upset people with the things that upset them.

Prayer jotter

Do you ever think you shouldn't do something, but you do it anyway? Or maybe you realize straight after doing it? This is called being aware of your sin, as King David was. Write or draw a sorry prayer to God.

Right and wrong

Looking back

What is the most beautiful thing you've seen? Thank God for your eyes.

Your eyes might not work very well. If so, ask God to show you his world in a different way.

To do

Can you decide which of these pictures show someone doing the right thing and which the wrong thing? Tick the right things and put a cross by the wrong ones.

To talk about

Is it always easy to tell what is right and wrong? How do you decide if what you do or someone else does is right or wrong?

What happens when you do the wrong thing?

Explore the Bible

People are filled with all kinds of wickedness; they are full of jealousy. They gossip and speak evil of one another; they are insolent and boastful; they disobey their parents; they do not keep their promises, and they show no kindness for others.

Romans 1:29–31

When people do certain things wrong, they may get arrested by the police. Then they have to go and see a judge in a court, who has to decide what punishment they should get. Sometimes this is a fine (they have to pay money) or they might go to prison.

This verse tells us some of the wrong things people do. Do you think that doing wrong things deserves a punishment?

Prayer jotter

Is doing the right thing always the easiest thing to do? It is made harder when all your friends seem to be doing the wrong thing.

Ask God to help you make good choices about how to behave well. Write a prayer and draw a picture.

Not so perfect

Looking back

Who is the oldest person you know? What is the difference between you and them? What things are the same?

Thank God for that person and ask him to be with them.

To do

Look at these words and pictures. Circle the ones that *everyone* does at some time in their life. Leave the ones that only some people do.

To talk about

Do you know anyone who is perfect?

Perhaps there is someone you know about in history who did really good things. Do you think they ever did anything wrong?

Ask the person you are sharing this book with whether either of you has ever done anything wrong.

Explore the Bible

> **The Lord looks down from heaven at human beings to see if there are any who are wise. But they have all gone wrong.**
>
> *Psalm 14:2 and 3*

There are some things that only a few people can or will do—like owning a dog or watching a football match. Some things everyone will do—like washing their hands or drinking water.

This verse tells us that there is something else that everyone will do—wrong things. The only person in the history of the world who didn't ever upset God was Jesus. He was perfect and didn't do anything wrong.

Prayer jotter

Look at today's verse from the book of Psalms. Can you draw a picture of the problem that is made between us and God when we do wrong things?

Because of God's love

Looking back

Have you done anything naughty in the last few days?

Think to yourself about things that maybe no one else saw you do. Did God know you did those things? Did they make him happy?

Say sorry to him now.

To talk about

Have you learnt at school about why things happen? For example, have you learnt about why seeds grow? Maybe you have learnt about why we have to do certain things at certain times—for example, why we should be polite to visitors.

Try to think of other things you have learnt about at school that help you understand why things happen.

To do

Finish these sentences.

I wash before a meal because

Ducks swim well because

I don't jump off high things because

Explore the Bible

For God loved the world so much that he gave his only Son, so that everyone who believes in him may not die but have eternal life.

John 3:16

God loves us so much that he really wants to make it possible for us not to be separated from him because we do things wrong. Because of his love for us, he wants to make things right between us.

Over the next six sessions, we are going to think about forgiveness—God's way of sorting out the problem of the things we do wrong.

Prayer jotter

How does it make you feel to know that God wants to sort out the problem of the wrong things we do? Tell God how you feel here.

Maybe you could draw a love heart and decorate it to remind you of God's love for us.

Washed clean

Looking back

How many different birds do you know?

How many different animals can you name?

Thank God that he made his creation so varied and interesting.

To talk about

When you water seeds, what happens?

When you wash dirty clothes, what happens?

When you wind up a toy, what happens?

Explore the Bible

Remove my sin, and I will be clean; wash me, and I will be whiter than snow.

Psalm 51:7

The word for God taking away sins (the things we do wrong) is 'forgiveness'. Here we read that King David is asking for God's forgiveness. He is saying that to be forgiven is like being washed clean by God.

Before forgiveness, our sins are like dirt clinging to us. After we are forgiven by God, it's as if we are made clean.

To do

Link these pictures to show 'before' and 'after'.

Prayer jotter

When God forgives us, the things we do wrong go away completely. There is no sign of them left. Do you need God to forgive you? Ask him to, and then write down how it feels to be washed clean by God's forgiveness.

New on the inside

Looking back

Look at the things that belong to you.

Some children don't have very much. Pray that God will provide all they need. Thank him for your things.

To talk about

Look around where you are now.

Are there any cupboards or boxes with things inside? Can you remember what is inside each cupboard or box or drawer?

How many things with an inside can you think of or see?

Explore the Bible

Create a pure heart in me, O God, and put a new and loyal spirit in me.

Psalm 51:10

Cupboards and drawers are not the only things that have stuff inside! People have an inside as well.

What's inside you? Hopefully there are some lungs to help you breathe, kidneys and a liver to sort out your blood, and a heart to keep you alive.

Some people say that your heart is also a symbol of where your feelings come from. Perhaps it is where the desire to do wrong things comes from too. It is because our heart is in the very middle of our body that people say that. What do you think?

This verse tells us that when we are forgiven, our inside heart is made clean. We are washed on the inside as well as on the outside.

To do

Here are some things that are closed. Can you guess what's on the inside?

Prayer jotter

When God cleans up our inside heart by forgiving us, he wants us to do right things, not wrong things. Write or draw here what your inside heart is feeling about God.

Tell God

Looking back

What made you sad today? Pray about it.

What made you happy today? Thank God for it.

To talk about

Who have you talked to today? What did you talk about to each of them?

What good news have you told someone recently? Have you ever had to tell someone some bad news?

To do

Here are some people talking. What do you think they are talking about?

Explore the Bible

If we say that we have no sin, we deceive ourselves, and there is no truth in us. But if we confess our sins to God, he will keep his promise and do what is right: he will forgive us our sins and purify us from all our wrongdoing.

1 John 1:8 and 9

We talk about a lot of things, don't we? We chat about funny things, sad things, things we have done and things we are planning to do.

God wants us to talk to him. He wants to hear about our lives, but he also wants to hear about the things we do wrong so that he can forgive us. The Bible uses the word 'confess'. Maybe you have heard that word in church as well. It means to tell God the things you have done wrong. He won't be cross with you—he wants to forgive you and make you clean.

Prayer jotter

It's not easy telling another person that you did something wrong. Imagine confessing to a teacher that you spoilt something in your class.

God wants us to confess to him the things we do wrong. We needn't be worried: God loves us and wants to forgive us. Tell him about your day now.

Forgive others

Looking back

Is there a place that you've heard about in the world where people are sad and hurt? Pray for the people trying to help them. Pray that they will be wise and do the right thing to help.

To talk about

Can you remember any nasty things that have been done to you? Has anything like that happened in the last few days? What did it feel like?

How do you think and feel about the person who was nasty to you now?

Explore the Bible

Forgive us the wrongs we have done, as we forgive the wrongs that others have done to us.

Matthew 6:12

God wants us to show love to other people. He even wants us to show love to people who have upset and hurt us.

This verse is from the Lord's Prayer—maybe you know the rest of it. Have you heard it at church? Jesus taught the prayer to teach us about how God wants us to live.

It's not always easy to forgive others. Try to remember how you feel when God forgives you. Make someone else feel like that by forgiving them.

To do

Here are some pictures of children saying sorry to each other. Can you work out what has happened and who needs to forgive whom?

Prayer jotter

Is there someone you need to forgive? It might feel scary, but ask God to give you courage to do it. Draw that person here.

Keep on forgiving

Looking back

Think about the people you love. What do you love about them?

Thank God for them. Ask God to keep them safe.

To talk about

What things do you have to keep doing over and over again? Maybe something you find hard to learn and need to practise—playing a musical instrument or doing something physical like a forward roll or handstand.

Can you think of other things?

Explore the Bible

Then Peter came to Jesus and asked, 'Lord, if my brother keeps on sinning against me, how many times do I have to forgive him? Seven times?' 'No, not seven times,' answered Jesus, 'but seventy times seven.'

Matthew 18:21 and 22

Have you ever had someone keep on doing the same nasty thing to you? Maybe you know someone else who has.

Jesus told Peter that he should forgive 'seventy times seven'. He didn't actually mean Peter to keep a count. He was using that really big number to show us that we need to keep on forgiving people. We keep on forgiving people, for ever, without stopping.

To do

Here are people doing things that they have practised over and over again.

Which would you want to do? Which would you find easy to do?

Prayer jotter

Forgiving people this much is quite difficult. We need God's special power, the Holy Spirit, to help us to do it. Ask him now for help.

Draw someone who has been forgiven.

God teaches us to forgive

Looking back

Pray for people who are ill in hospital. Perhaps you know someone who is there. Pray that God would help the doctors and nurses to make them better.

To talk about

Who sets you an example? What do they show you? Who teaches you how to do things? Is it only your schoolteacher?

Do you set an example to anyone? Who? What do you show them?

Explore the Bible

Be tolerant with one another and forgive one another whenever any of you has a complaint against someone else. You must forgive one another just as the Lord has forgiven you.

Colossians 3:13

Forgiveness is one of the things that God is brilliant at. We've seen that over the last few sessions. He cleans us up on the inside and outside and takes our sins away.

We might find it harder to forgive others than God does to forgive us. But it says in this verse that we must follow his example and do as he has done to us by forgiving people.

To do

What is being taught to the children in these pictures? Can you draw another one?

Prayer jotter

Jesus' life gives us the best example of how to live. Think of things that Jesus teaches us to do. Ask God to help you learn and live Jesus' way.

Betrayed and arrested

Looking back

Think about school. Think of the really good things about it. Thank God for those things.

Think about the bits you don't enjoy so much. Ask God to help you with those things.

To talk about

Have you ever met a policeman or woman? Maybe your family knows someone who does that as a job. Or maybe you had a visit from a police officer while at school. What would you say their job is all about?

Explore the Bible

Judas had given the crowd a signal: 'The man I kiss is the one you want.' As soon as Judas arrived, he went up to Jesus and said 'Teacher!' and kissed him. So they arrested Jesus and held him tight.

Mark 14:44–46

Jesus had never done anything wrong. But he still had enemies. The people in charge at the time didn't like him teaching about God's kingdom. The people in charge wanted to arrest him.

Poor Jesus, betrayed by a friend and arrested for doing nothing wrong!

To do

Here are some people who have done a wrong thing. Which of them will be arrested by the policewoman here?

Prayer jotter

Keeping the law of the land is a difficult job. The police do a hard job.

Draw a police officer here and pray for them to make good decisions and for God to keep them safe.

They told lies

Looking back

Think about your friends. How well did you play together in the day just gone? Did anyone fall out with anyone else? What was it all about? Did you do the right thing?

Ask God to help you do the right thing with your friends.

To talk about

Do you know what lies are? Perhaps you can think of a lie right now? It might be something silly like 'All cows are pink!'

Why are lies wrong, particularly when they are about people or about something that has happened? Are lies ever told at your school? How does it feel if someone lies about you?

To do

Put a tick by the true statements and a cross by the lies.

The earth is square

A baby swan is called a cygnet

Eating loads of chocolate for every meal is good for you

It never rains in the summer

Explore the Bible

> **The chief priests and the whole Council tried to find some evidence against Jesus in order to put him to death, but they could not find any. Many witnesses told lies against Jesus, but their stories did not agree.**
>
> *Mark 14:55 and 56*

The people in charge wanted to get rid of Jesus by accusing him of a crime that they could punish him for. They tried to find something he had done wrong, but they couldn't. They even told lies to try to accuse him, but even the lies didn't make a difference. Jesus had done nothing wrong.

Prayer jotter

Jesus had never done anything wrong. This is because he is holy, like God his Father. You might like to draw a picture of Jesus before the council.

Who are you?

Looking back

Think about the people you know. Is anyone ill or upset at the moment? Ask God to be with them and help them to get better.

To talk about

If you met someone new right now, how would you introduce yourself to them? What would you say to describe yourself? What do you like doing?

How would you introduce your friends?

Explore the Bible

But Jesus kept quiet and would not say a word. Again the High Priest questioned him, 'Are you the Messiah, the Son of the Blessed God?' 'I am,' answered Jesus. The High Priest said, 'You heard his blasphemy. What is your decision?' They all voted against him: he was guilty and should be put to death.

Mark 14:61–64

Blasphemy is when you say something against God. The priests thought that Jesus was lying about who he said he was. 'How could he be the Son of God?' they asked. We know that he was, but they hadn't understood what Jesus had taught about the kingdom of heaven. They had seen his miracles but hadn't seen them as a sign from God.

Jesus stood quietly. He knew he was God's Son—even though they didn't believe it.

To do

Many hundreds of years before Jesus was even born, a man called Isaiah wrote about a servant who would come to die. If you have a Bible, you might like to look up Isaiah 53:7–9. Remember these words over the next few sessions. See if you can see the other parts of these verses that came true.

Prayer jotter

The High Priest wanted to know who Jesus was. Can you think of words you would use to describe him? Write them here and use them as a prayer to praise Jesus for who he is and what he is like.

Confused friend

Looking back

Is there anything you find difficult at the moment? Why is it hard?

God cares about you so much that he wants to help you. Ask God to help you with that difficult thing.

To talk about

What are your friends like? What are the best things about them? Do you think they would stand up for you if things got difficult? Have they ever stood up for you in the past?

To do

Here's a picture of Peter. Colour it in and fill in the gaps in the words to describe what sort of friend he was to Jesus.

L _ y _ l H e _ p f _ _

A l w _ _ s t _ _ r e

H _ n _ s t

Explore the Bible

> **Peter was in the courtyard when one of the High Priest's servant girls came by. When she saw Peter, she looked straight at him and said, 'You, too, were with Jesus of Nazareth.' But he denied it. 'I don't know... I don't understand what you are talking about,' he answered.**
>
> *Mark 14:66–68*

Poor Peter. What had happened? He used to be loyal, helpful, always there and honest. What had happened now? He couldn't even admit he knew who Jesus was.

Poor Peter—he was confused and sad and angry and frightened. What would happen to Jesus?

Prayer jotter

Think about how Jesus felt, being let down by his friend. Think about how you will be a good friend always. Write a prayer asking God to help you.

Questions

Looking back

Some people don't have homes or beds. Pray that God would help them through other people.

Some people don't have any friends. Pray that God will be their friend.

To do

Play the 'Yes/No game'. The object of the game is for you to avoid saying 'yes' or 'no'. If you say either of those words, you are out. Try to get someone to say 'yes' or 'no' by asking them questions. See if you can catch them out. Then swap round.

To talk about

We learn about people by asking them questions. What sort of questions do you use to find out about people? What are you interested to find out about in the people you meet?

Explore the Bible

Pilate questioned him, 'Are you the King of the Jews?' Jesus answered, 'So you say.' The chief priests were accusing Jesus of many things, so Pilate questioned him again, 'Aren't you going to answer?' Again Jesus refused to say a word, and Pilate was amazed.

Mark 15:2–5

It might seem strange to us that Jesus didn't reply to Pilate—he was the Roman Governor in charge of the whole country. The questions seem simple enough, but Jesus didn't say 'yes' or 'no'.

Jesus didn't need to answer the questions. He didn't need to try to save himself from the punishment, even though he was innocent. He knew that he had to die. Keep on reading this book to find out why!

Prayer jotter

Have you any questions you'd like to ask God? Maybe there are things you don't understand about the world or about why things happen. Write them or draw about them here.

Sent to die

Looking back

Think about the day just gone. What was the funniest bit? Thank God for it.

What was the most exciting bit? Thank God for it.

What was the scariest bit? Thank God for being with you and making you brave.

To talk about

Do you ever think about the future? What sort of job do you want to do when you grow up?

How far ahead in your life do you think you know about? Do you know what your next school will be?

Do you think we can ever be really sure about what is in the future?

To do

Guess what these children want to be in the future.

Explore the Bible

Pilate spoke to the crowd, 'What, then, do you want me to do with the one they call the King of the Jews?' They shouted back, 'Crucify him!'

Mark 15:12 and 13

This seems like a terrible end to the story of Jesus' life. The people in charge wanted Jesus dead because they didn't like what he said and did. But we know that he had never done anything wrong.

However, Jesus knew that he would have to die—it was the purpose of his life. He knew his Father God had a big plan for him and that dying was part of that plan. Jesus grew up knowing he must die in this way.

Prayer jotter

Being a friend of God means we don't have to worry about what will happen in the future, because we know that God will be with us. Sometimes bad things happen, but as long as we trust God to be with us, even the bad times are OK.

Pray that God will always be with you and your family.

Jesus is teased

Looking back

Is there anything really exciting at the moment? Maybe it's something still to come or that you are involved with at school.

Tell God why it's exciting and ask him to be with you while you wait for it to happen.

To talk about

Have you ever had people tease you and say nasty things about you? How did it make you feel?

Have you ever teased someone? Do you think that was the right thing to do?

To do

Which of these children is doing the right thing to stop bullies hurting them?

Explore the Bible

They beat him over the head with a stick, spat on him, fell on their knees, and bowed down to him. When they had finished mocking him, they took off the purple robe and put his own clothes back on him. Then they led him out to crucify him.

Mark 15:19 and 20

Poor Jesus. This was an awful thing to happen to him. He was hurt by the stick and hurt by the mocking names. They were teasing him because they didn't understand. They were being nasty because they thought they had to do it to please the people in charge. Poor Jesus, he was all alone and was being hurt.

Some people in this world wonder why others get hurt. They especially wonder why God doesn't stop them getting hurt. Often the things we wonder about God can never have an answer. Perhaps, though, we can look at Jesus suffering at the hands of bullies and remember that when we suffer or are hurt, Jesus knows what it feels like. He has suffered too.

Prayer jotter

When we feel alone and hurt as Jesus must have felt, we can talk to him about it.

Imagine you feel sad now. Write what you would say to him. Next time you do feel sad, you can use the words as a prayer.

Jesus dies

Looking back

When did you last play outdoors? What did you do? Did you have fun?

Thank God for the outdoors and for all you can do there.

To talk about

Have you known anyone who has died? Was it perhaps a relative or family friend? Maybe you have had a pet that died. Talk about what it feels like when someone dies.

To do

Here are some pictures. How are they connected to what happens when someone dies?

Explore the Bible

They took Jesus to a place called Golgotha, which means 'The Place of the Skull'. There they tried to give him wine mixed with a drug called myrrh, but Jesus would not drink it. Then they crucified him and divided his clothes among themselves. At noon the whole country was covered with darkness. With a loud cry Jesus died.

Mark 15:22–24, 33 and 37

We usually remember these events on Good Friday. Why do we call it 'good' when it's about something so awful and sad? Jesus died young and in a terrible way. His friends were frightened and lonely. Why is this good?

Jesus knew he had to die and so did God. Jesus died to sort out the problem of sin in people and in the world. Some people say that 'Good Friday' is really 'God's Friday'. But how does this horrible day end in such good news? Keep reading to find out!

Prayer jotter

Today's verses seem awful, don't they? However, through it all, God was in charge. Sometimes we feel awful too. Thank God that he is always in charge, whether times are good or bad!

Jesus is buried

Looking back

Sometimes we say or do things that upset other people. Has this happened to you lately? Do you need to say sorry to anyone when you next see them?

Say sorry to God about it now and ask him to help you when you apologize.

To do

Here are some ways in which people show their love. Look at each picture. Who would you show love to in this way?

To talk about

Think of the people that you love. What is the best way to show you love them? Remember that each might be different. When did you last show love to these people? How do they show you that they love you?

Explore the Bible

> **Joseph of Arimathea bought a linen sheet, took Jesus' body down, wrapped it in the sheet, and placed it in a tomb which had been dug out of solid rock. Then he rolled a large stone across the entrance to the tomb.**
>
> *Mark 15:46*

Jesus had died and all his friends were surprised and frightened.

But Joseph of Arimathea showed that he loved Jesus, in a very practical way. He had a tomb that belonged to his family. He took Jesus' dead body and put it there. It was the right thing to do to show his love for Jesus.

Prayer jotter

Jesus' friends must have been really sad that Jesus had died. They would be mourning him. Do you know anyone who is mourning someone who has died? (Maybe you are.) Pray for God to comfort them.

Draw something here that you could give to show that you love them.

Sunday morning

Looking back

What made you laugh in the last few days? How does it feel when you laugh? Do you like it?

Thank God for friends and for laughter.

To talk about

How does it feel to be not looking forward to something? Have you ever felt like that? What were you not looking forward to? What did it feel like when you had done it?

Explore the Bible

Very early on Sunday morning, at sunrise, Mary Magdalene, Mary and Salome went to the tomb. On the way they said to one another, 'Who will roll away the stone from the entrance to the tomb?' (It was a very large stone.) Then they looked up and saw that the stone had already been rolled back.

Mark 16:2–4

It was Saturday night. Mary, Mary and Salome were so sad that their friend Jesus had died. They knew Jesus' body had to be prepared for his proper funeral. They were going to go and do that early on the Sunday morning. They must have been dreading it.

But when they arrived, they had another shock. The tomb was empty and Jesus' body had gone. They were really surprised! Where had he gone? Where was Jesus?

To do

Here's a picture of that Sunday morning for you to colour.

Prayer jotter

Often we dread something—we think it will be awful and we would rather not do it. But often we get a surprise and it isn't as bad as we expect. Ask God to be with you in the things you dread. Ask him to surprise you with something nice in the awful situation.

Back to life!

Looking back

What did you do in the day just gone? Did you learn anything new? What was it?

Thank God that you can think and learn and remember.

To do

Link these pictures with a line to show the order in which you do things through the day.

To talk about

Have you ever been so surprised by something you have hardly believed it could be true? Maybe a really great present? Or a fantastic family surprise? Think of something and remember how you reacted. What did it feel like?

Explore the Bible

After Jesus rose from death early on Sunday, he appeared first to Mary Magdalene. She went and told his companions. They were mourning and crying; and when they heard her say that Jesus was alive and that she had seen him, they did not believe her.

Mark 16:9–11

After Jesus had risen from the dead, he wanted Mary to be the first to know. Then he wanted everyone else to know too—first his close friends, the disciples, and then the rest of the world!

Mary must have been bursting with excitement, but the disciples were full of doom and gloom. They were still so shocked that Jesus had died at all, they couldn't now believe he was alive again.

Prayer jotter

Mary learnt something new and amazing about Jesus. He had come back to life! When you learn something new about Jesus, think about who you would tell. Draw them here and remember to tell them!

Week 4
Session 6

The disciples believe

Looking back

What is your most favourite place in the whole world? When did you go there? Why is it your favourite place? Thank God for what makes it so good.

To do

Possible or impossible? Which of these things is impossible to do? Do you think any might happen in the future?

To talk about

Can you think of things that are impossible to do? What about jumping to the moon or walking all the way to school on your hands?

In the past, people would have thought it was impossible to do some of the things we do today. For example, talking on the phone, using the Internet, flying in an aeroplane.

Explore the Bible

> **Last of all, Jesus appeared to the eleven disciples as they were eating. He scolded them, because they did not have faith and because they were too stubborn to believe those who had seen him alive.**
>
> *Mark 16:14*

We see here that the disciples had to believe the impossible. Here was Jesus, alive again, standing with them. It's not easy believing the impossible. But believing that Jesus came back to life and is still alive now is at the very middle of being a Christian. We don't have to worry about anything because God is the God of the impossible!

Prayer jotter

Jesus didn't stay dead. Hurrah! Over the next few days, we will find out what his death and resurrection have to do with the problem of our doing wrong things. For now, think of some praise words to describe how it feels to know Jesus is alive again.

Jesus makes the difference

Looking back

What is your favourite animal? What's good about it? Thank God for that animal.

To talk about

What do you do when you break up with friends? How do you try to sort it out? Does it always work out OK? Are there children you are no longer friends with? Why is that?

Explore the Bible

> **At one time you were far away from God and were his enemies because of the evil things you did and thought. But now, by means of the physical death of his Son, God has made you his friends, in order to bring you, holy, pure, and faultless, into his presence.**
>
> *Colossians 1:21 and 22*

Perhaps you remember, at the beginning of this book we talked about the things we do wrong separating us from God. Because of his holiness (being pure and clean), it is impossible for anything bad or wrong to come near him.

This verse says that being separated from God is like being God's enemies. When people are enemies, they keep apart from each other.

Jesus' death was like the punishment for all the things we all do wrong. It is because of Jesus that we can now be friends with God—we are no longer kept separate.

To do

Here are three pictures that might help you to understand how Jesus' death helped sort out the problem of sin. Perhaps you could colour them.

Prayer jotter

Today's verse tells us that when we go to God now, it is as pure, holy and faultless people. Our sins no longer matter. Praise God that we can now come directly to him as friends. Thank him that we are no longer enemies.

Now we are friends

Looking back

What is your favourite type of weather? Thank God for the weather (even the bits you don't like).

To talk about

Have you ever been given a problem to sort out?

How do you sort out problems? If things look difficult, how do you tackle them?

To do

Here are some problems. Can you work them out?

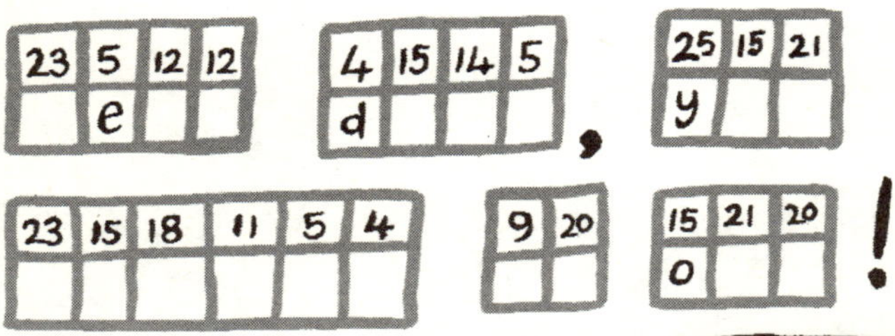

Explore the Bible

We were God's enemies, but he made us his friends through the death of his Son. Now that we are God's friends, how much more will we be saved by Christ's life! But that is not all; we rejoice because of what God has done through our Lord Jesus Christ, who has now made us God's friends.

Romans 5:10 and 11

Now we know that God doesn't want to be our enemy. He wants to sort it out. And because of Jesus, we can now call ourselves God's friends. We can do all the things that friends do, like talking and sharing things together.

We learnt earlier in the book about forgiveness and how only God can clean us up and give us a new inside heart through his forgiveness. It is because of Jesus' death that we can have that forgiveness. God still dislikes the things we do wrong; he still wants us to tell him about those things. We get cleaned up by God because we are his friends. That is really good news, isn't it?

Prayer jotter

Being a friend of Jesus is not really about what we do. It's about what God does for us. Do you believe that Jesus forgives you when you ask? If you do, you are a Christian.

Perhaps you would like to ask God to come and be in your life, helping you to believe and to live for him in every way.

The old has gone

Looking back

If you were to look out of the window, what would you see? What is the most beautiful bit? Thank God for that.

To talk about

Look around your room. Can you see anything that is new? Was it new to replace something old or was it completely new? If it replaced something old, why did that thing need replacing?

Can you think of anything else your family has that is new and replaced something old? What is it like to get something new?

Explore the Bible

Anyone who is joined to Christ is a new being; the old is gone, the new has come. All this is done by God, who through Christ changed us from enemies into his friends and gave us the task of making others his friends also.

2 Corinthians 5:17 and 18

Being forgiven by God is an amazing thing! It not only cleans us up by taking away the things we do wrong; it also gives us a fresh start. All the old things can go—we have a new life being friends with Jesus.

God has planned to keep on forgiving us. He knows that we will still do things wrong. He just wants us to say sorry so that he can forgive us again. We can make a new start every day with God as our friend, rather than as our enemy!

To do

Link the pictures to show the new and the old together.

Prayer jotter

Are there things that you do wrong that seem to keep on happening? Sometimes it is hard to break old habits.

Write or draw those things here and ask God to come and be with you to help you to do things differently.

A new place to be

Looking back

Look at your face in a mirror. If you are reading this with someone else, look carefully at each other's faces. Look at the detail; try to count freckles or marks; look at the different colours.

Isn't God an amazing creator to make our faces just as they are? Praise and thank him.

To talk about

What do you think heaven will be like? What do you think it might look like?

We know that it will be great. Think about what and who would need to be there to make it great for you.

Explore the Bible

Then I saw a new heaven and a new earth. The first heaven and the first earth disappeared, and the sea vanished.

Revelation 21:1

No living person has ever been to heaven and come back to earth. We don't know exactly what it will be like because no one has seen it. However, from the Bible we can get some understanding of what it is like.

We can see here that it will be brand new. There will be nothing old or tired or broken. Even people will be made completely new—no one will be ill or in pain.

This verse tells us that the sea will have disappeared. The reason it says this is that in biblical times, people thought that the sea was where chaos came from. Chaos leads to accidents and danger. In heaven, everything will be perfect. There won't be any room for chaos.

To do

Jesus spoke to his disciples about heaven. If you have a Bible, you might like to look up John 14:1 and 2. What does the writer say heaven will be like? Try to draw what heaven will look like. Remember that it is where God lives.

Prayer jotter

Perhaps you would like to tell God the things from this earth that you would like to see in the new heaven and earth. Maybe there are things you definitely don't want to see! Perhaps you could make a list of them here. Then ask God to sort out the best for everyone.

Together with God

Looking back

Who do you live with? Think of each person. Talk to God about them, maybe asking him to look after them or to help them with something that troubles them. God cares for them. Thank him that he does.

To talk about

Do you have any friends or family whom you don't see very often because they live a long way away? What are they like? Why do you like seeing them?

What is it like when you meet up? When you meet them after a long time apart, what is it like?

Explore the Bible

> **'Now God's home is with human beings! He will live with them, and they shall be his people. God himself will be with them, and he will be their God.'**
>
> *Revelation 21:3*

We have found out in this book about how wrong things separate us from God. Being apart from God is a bit like us having a part missing, like a teddy without an eye or a bike without a wheel. But we have also found out that because of Jesus we can be forgiven and become God's friends again. It is because of Jesus' Easter experience that we will finally meet with God in heaven and be with him for ever. It will be like being at home with him—which is exactly where God always wanted us to be!

To do

Here are some things that have a part of them missing. What is missing?

Prayer jotter

Heaven is the place where we will see God our heavenly Father and Jesus his Son face to face. What do you imagine that will be like? What will you do, and how will you react?

Perhaps you could draw a picture of yourself meeting God in heaven.